MENTAL FLOSS

Hattie Hatstar

Published by Green Feather Books 2016

Copyright ©Hattie Hatstar 2016

All rights reserved

This book is sold subject to the condition that it shall not, by way of trade or otherwise, be lent, resold, hired out or otherwise circulated in any form or binding other than that in which it is published without the publisher's prior written consent and without a similar condition being imposed on the subsequent purchaser

ISBN 978-0-9574777-1-1

Green Feather Books
The Studio
The Nelson Arms
Main Street
Middleton
Matlock
DE4 4LU

This book is dedicated to you the reader. Without your support I'd have to go and get a shit job I don't want.

Introduction

This book is a collection of words that I've written over the last 25 years. The first section was written in London, when I was young, irreverent and just working out what I liked. London was a vibrant and affordable place to live in the early 90's, further education was still funded and I was doing a degree at the Camberwell College of Art. I was having a whale of a time coming across such radical ideals as squatting, free parties and road protesting for the first time, whilst not accumulating 37 grands worth of debt. This section is entitled "Old Life", it suddenly seems like a long time ago.

In 1995, after a couple of trips to Twyford Down, a really mental Claremont Road eviction and a cosmic dawn at Glastonbury Festival where I came to my senses at sunrise with my arms around a horse, I sold everything I owned, hitch-hiked to the west country and moved into a Beech tree at a place called Fairmile, where a group of people were protesting about the A30 bypass being built. This is where the "Tree Life" section my book was written. I'd never lived anywhere as beautiful as that, or had friends that I loved as much as that. It was a special, beautiful, fairly traumatic moment in time that will never occur again.[1]

After Fairmile I didn't live anywhere for years, or rather I lived everywhere, various benders[2] in various woods, different continents, a horse drawn wagon, a shepherd's hut, a ditch or 2 and a lot of sofas. I was writing all the time and doing whatever work came my way. In the late 90's I learnt to play the accordion, started to write songs, earnt enough money to buy a truck and then went on permanent tour busking on the streets of Europe and playing gigs and festivals everywhere. All the words from this time are in the

---

1. Twyford Down and Claremont Road were both road protest sites, so was Fairmile. If you don't know anything about it do an internet search for 'road protesting 1990's' or look at http://www.cartoonkate.co.uk/copse/

2. A sort of primitive tent. If you want to know more, type "how to build a bender" into a search engine

section "Wild Life". It was wild, I really enjoyed it.

In 2002 the inevitable happened. I got pregnant, broke my truck and moved back to England where I lived with the circus for a bit, then in a massive caravan in the West Country. Pregnancy, motherhood and babies make for a lot of song material – that's the section entitled "New Life".

The last section of the book brings us up to now. The relentlessness of life makes for a lot of songs and the occasional poem. Everything is in there, life, death, love, optimism and misery.

Here's to being free for another 25 years.

Hattie Hatstar
January 2016.

Contents

Old Life (London 1991-1995) 11
Sheep and beards 12
Stupid question 13
Time 14
Chocolate 15
Sport 16
Daydream on the bus 17
Offensive square box poem 18
Need a boy 19
Word puzzle obsessive talks herself out of having an affair 20
Sheep 21
Health kick 22
What the doctors say 23
Pet maintenance 24
Stop rewind 25
Rumination 26
Surfacing 27

Tree Life (1995-1997) 29
Between us the moon and the fire 30
Toad's lament 31
Evening 32
Poem in the dark 33
Dawn (city) 34
Dawn (tree) 35
Little dinner poem 36
Moron Poem 37
Sad 38

Not that far 39

Homeless 40

Wild life (1997-2002).. 41

Frog is 42

Start a fight 43

Up your arse 44

Girl thing 46

Mankind 47

Valium holiday 48

I free 49

Fags 50

Formica 52

Evil twin 54

Himalayas 56

Hippy song 57

Blagging 58

Boyfriends 59

Supermarket song 60

What is going on? 61

Gardening job 62

Sailing By 63

NIMBY 64

Love poem 65

New life (2002-2007) 67

Pregnant 68

Baby song 69

I want to give birth to a clanger. 70

I want my brain back 71

Duck cow tractor	72
Sweat shop	74
Home on the range	76
Relentless life (2008-2015)	**77**
This land is…	78
New nuclear	79
Diamond geezer	80
Garden shed not bloodshed	81
The B.N.P. song	82
CCTV	84
Real love song	85
Stop it	86
Forty and fat	88
Car boot sale	90
Fit for Armageddon	92
Idioms	94
February Poem	96
Don't Google that lump	97
I know	98
Come run away with me	99

Old Life
(London 1991-1995)

Sheep and beards

They say that life is weird
But so are sheep and beards.

Stupid question

Where do you come from?
I don't know
Inside maybe,
Outside, outer space
The other side of the moon.
Biologically I come from my father's seed
Grown in my mother's womb,
Geographically a town too near to London to be worth counting,
Fanatically I was either spewed from hell
Or fresh from God's sperm fountain.
But here I am
Regardless of where I started,
Come from the whole world,
Made up of all its yesterdays and tomorrows
Just now,
So I don't suppose I come from anywhere in particular.

Time

Once upon a time
There was no time
Except night time
And day time,
Then somebody put numbers where the sun was
And time became endless
Instead of just here and now time.
Time began to pass,
Sometimes slowly
Sometimes fast,
Sometimes there wasn't enough time,
Other times
Time was vast.
There became a time to live
And a time to die,
And an old father time
With his beady eye
On those who
Though they were watching time fly,
Might not notice
Their time to die.
People learnt all about the beginning of time
But became afraid about the end,
Because to them endings were sad
Even though those they left behind
Had time yet to live,
And when they died
Their time wasn't really up,
It just became timeless
Like it was
Once upon a time,
When there was only night time
And day time,
Before anyone had put numbers
Where the sun was.

Chocolate

I like chocolate when I'm sad
Or when I'm full of joy,
I like chocolate when life's bad
I like chocolate more than boys,
I like chocolate at the daybreak
I like chocolate in the night,
I'll eat chocolate til my jaw breaks
Cos chocolate is alright.

Sport

Earth words cannot report
How much I fucking hate sport.
It's so boring and pointless
Why? Why?
I want to blow sport sky high.

Daydream on the bus

In my daydream on the bus
You turned to me and said
My dear I love you truly
And will do so til I'm dead,

My body tingled to my toes
My astonished mouth did drop,
You threw me down
Removed my clothes
Oh shit I've missed my stop.

Offensive square box poem

Look at me
I'm happy,
Sitting in my square box home,
Watching my square box T.V.
And eating my square box T.V. dinner,
Which I brought home from a box shaped Supermarket,
In a square box,
On a square bus.

I only like flowers
That come in square boxes,
I only like vegetables
Packaged and clean,

I have wipe clean
White Formica
Wet dreams

About square boxes
Fucking,
From the prison cell of my home,

What does
It mean?

NB. This poem turned into the Formica song 5 years later - see p.52

Need a boy

Need a boy to make me angry
Need a boy to make me sad
Need a boy to make me feel
Like I am going mad.

Need a boy to hang around
Need a boy that I can hit
Need a boy to be abusive
Stupid boys are full of shit.

Need a boy to do my head in
Need a boy to do my back
Need a stupid boy to play with
Stupid boy is what I lack.

Word puzzle obsessive talks herself out of having an affair

David and Ben together make bed,
Den
Bad vibe
Evaded,
Idea!
Most obviously they make bed
But I think I like den best.
Although they could be a dab hand at dividing beads,
Bending Danes,
Joining bands and vending Dads,
I bid
Or have bidden them,
A most avid
Goodnight.

Sheep

I'll tell a little story
About a lovely sheep,
It will be fairly gory
And it won't send you to sleep.

Once there was a happy sheep
Living in a field,
Until a farmer came along
And said it must be killed.
"We want our chops
We want our roast
For us to eat on Sundays,
We need the bits
To spread on toast
And make a stew on Mondays"

The sheep it fled
It ran away
Upon its tiny feet,
But the farmer trapped it in a pen
And slaughtered it for meat,

But the sheep will find eternal life
In the great field
In the sky,
And the farmer will get cancer
Suffer horribly
Then die.

Health kick

To cure
Wednesday morning after
Free party weekend
Tonsil trouble,
Simply gargle with Lavazza and fags.

What the doctors say

The doctors say
I've got lots of things
That end in 'A'
One day they
Will all go away.

Pet maintenance

The night my brother died
So did Antonia's goldfish
She had lent me
To keep alive.

Luckily Goldie's death
 Paled into insignificance
Against the loss of my brothers head.
Antonia didn't complain one bit
When she came to collect the empty tank.
She even thanked me
For my pet maintenance
Although it was so shit.

Stop rewind

Here we go
Rewind,
Yesterday's dark
Chewing on night-time,
Wrap your body
Up in mine,
Stop.
Rewind.

Rumination

The world revolves
The I-Ching won't tell,
I ruminate in my room
And come to no conclusion.

The world revolves
The cards don't say much,
I ruminate in my room
And come to no conclusion.

The world revolves
Tinned fruit is revolting,
I ruminate in my room
And come to no conclusion.

The world revolves
I don't give a toss,
I ruminate in my room
And come to no conclusion.

The world revolves
Bollocks, shit, fuck,
Wank, tits.
I come to no conclusion.

Surfacing

Morning comes,
Sunlight shines through curtains
Then coffee like treacle
Warming my insides.
I wish the sun would slip back down
To the depths of the night,
Where the world is in slow motion
And we move like we're underwater,
Struggling through
The infinite blackness
Of love.

Tree Life
(1995-1997)

Between us the moon and the fire

Between us
The moon and the fire
We have everything.
Thousands of miles in which to roam,
Free as flames
In the wood smoked homes of our souls.

Toad's lament

"Oh no"
Said the struggling little toad
"Here's another nasty road
These human beings really don't care
They seem to build them everywhere"
(And to a toad that's most unfair),
For how can a toad
Cross a road
When it's had no training,
And it's often in the dark
And invariably it's raining?

But roads are getting plentiful
And toads are getting hit,
And toads are really beautiful
But roads are full of shit.

Evening

Evening and
Even the flowers
Had turned their backs on us,
So without a word
We lit the fire
To keep away nightmares
And slept,
Til the flames died
And the sun rose
With the first bird
And the trees wept spring sap
To wake us up,
And we were wild
And we ate the world for breakfast.

Poem in the dark

I want the teapot,
There it is
No it's not.

Dawn (city)

Six A.M. on Sunday morning
And it's winter
And it's warm
(What with the world heating up and all),
And the birds are trying to sing away
The streetlights and the concrete
So they can tell the time again
And land on earth.
And a pigeons eating chips
In the half light
Under a bridge.
And I wish I had eyes in the back of my head
And knives sticking out from my body,
And I'm scared
I'm scared
And all of this is mad
And wrong
And sick,
Because night is supposed to be calm
And dawn sacred.

Dawn (tree)

The sun is heading for this side of the planet
As the last cold of the night
Bites the back of my neck
Into a frenzy.
Wondering if the stars are fading
Or my eyesight's failing
For want of sleep,
And straining
To work out if it's city glow
Or sun coming.
Silence

The birds are
Taking breath enough
For their first song.

Little dinner poem

Wet wood
Brown Rice
Long time
Tastes nice.

Moron Poem

Sod being fluffy
The solution in the stars
Says kill all the morons
That drive around in cars,
Kill all the morons
Before they start to breed,
Kill all the morons
The ones that watch TV.
Go to the supermarket
Take a big gun
And extinguish all the morons
Each and every one,
Burn down their Bovis homes,
Mash their bovine brains,
Sod being fluffy
And get into
Moron pain.

Sad

One day our garden
Will become a war zone
And we will have nothing
Nowhere
A roof of sky
A blanket of air
And each other
And forever
To find
Somewhere
To come home

Not that far

Imagine each bird's song
As the sound
Of a car,
And choke on your future
It's not that far.

Remember
Time travels fast,
Your future is coming towards you
At about
80 miles an hour.

If you blink sometimes
You're suddenly face to face
With things that were
In the distance.

If you open your eyes
You can hear it
Eating a pathway of chaos
Into your heart,

It's not that far.

Homeless

When there is no home
To go home to,
And what you once knew is spread
Further than the stars,
No longer alive as it was.
When tears sing
And sap runs like blood,
Remember how spring
Feeds the world
With fire,
And the bite of your love
Will return
With the sun
As it once did.

Wild life
(1997-2002)

Frog is

Frog is in the puddle
Rabbit's in the fox
World is in the universe
Man is in his box,
Grass is made of green stuff
Bird is made of song
Fox is made of freedom
Man went wrong.

Start a fight

Well you've got artificial plants
Under artificial lights
And your future is expanding
To artificial heights,
You're genetically distorting
All the things that give us life
I think it's time to start a fight.

You're frying up my mind
Projecting blip-verts on my eyes
Tarmac-ing the countryside
And filling up the skies,
With your airwaves and your aeroplanes
And dodgy orange lights
I think it's time to start a fight.

Well the ozone is depleting
And the icebergs overheating
And the cod are getting cancer
From the toxic waste they're eating,
Turning forests into dustbowls
And running rivers dry
I think it's time to start a fight.

Up your arse

There should be a law
Against your life
Your Marks and Spencer meals
Your stupid wife.
There should be law
Against your mind,
But there's not a lot in it
That I can find.
There should be a law
Against Dire Straits,
Against playing golf,
Against your face,
Because you use Colgate toothpaste
And Radion Plus,
If they served you shit
In a restaurant
You wouldn't make a fuss,
You're so jolly nice
And so jolly middle class
I'd like to ram your nippy hatchback
Up your Arse.

You go to Ikea
To buy your shelves,
And your toilet gives off
Floral smells,
Your fridge is a GMO living hell
You've got the national anthem
As your front door bell,
You've got crap magazines
On your kitchen table,
And your telly and your phone
Are both on cable,
And your kids will grow up to be most unstable,
And you should get a life
But you're not quite able to.

Arrrggghhh.

There should be a law
Against your life,
There should be a law
Against your wife,
Because you use Colgate toothpaste
And Radion Plus,
If they served you shit
In a restaurant
You wouldn't make a fuss,
You're so jolly nice
And so jolly middle class
I'd like to ram your nippy hatchback
Up your Arse.

Girl thing

Drunk
Twelve
Talking to four
Boys
Under a tree
Behind a house
On the street
Of the street party,
Maybe V E day 1985
Or something to do
With the royal family.
Think the conversation
With the four boys
Under the tree
Had something to do with sexuality.
Too young to notice
And too drunk to care
I find myself upstairs
With three of the four boys,
Two (maybe three) years older than me.
No consent
Consequently
They fucked me
One after the other
Two of them were brothers
I don't remember number three.
I took refuge
In the drunk head
Attached to the girl
Arranged on the bed
Like she wasn't alive,
Who didn't cry out
Or move to defend herself
Until she was
Twenty-five.

Mankind

Ducks don't need to pay any moorings
And rats don't need to pay rent.
Bats they hold no truck with Tesco's
And bunnies don't grovel in lent.
Turtles don't need to set their alarm clocks
Birds don't have to use planes,
Penguins they don't bother with suntans
And we think mankind's got the brains.

Chipmunks don't have to visit the dentist
And cows don't have to wear shoes.
Spiders don't have to buy expensive climbing tat
Moles don't tune into the news.
Hedgehogs don't drive around in red sports cars
Glow-worms aren't plugged into the mains,
Tigers they don't bother with blenders
And we think mankind's got the brains.

Valium holiday

Hit rock bottom
It hurts
Like a bottomless well of tears.
Cop out
Take a Valium holiday
It helps,
Like filling the well up with concrete
So you can't
Fall in.

I free

I sit
I knit
I dig
I eat
I laugh
I shit
I love
I weep
I haul
I hold
I carry
I sleep
I worry
I think
I learn
I breathe
I give
I drink
I take
I talk
I shake
I cry
I fall
I walk
I live
I dance
I build
I work
I can
I am
Free

Fags

Well you have another fag
And then you have another drink
And you smoke a little spliff
And you have a little think,
And it's all twisted in your mind
And there's no escape to find
And you keep running into walls
And all the alleys turn out blind.
They never taught you knots at school
So you can't tie a noose,
And you can't afford a shotgun
And Bic razors just won't do it,
And the oven is electric
And you haven't got a car,
The trains are unreliable
The nearest cliff to far,
So just have another fag
Oh they're worse for you than scag,
And you'll die horribly
A coughing cursing hag.

When the light of morning comes
You see the contents of your lungs,
And while you're gagging
You realise that you've smoked tonnes,
You must have smoked about a billion
And it costs you loads of pounds
And then there's the added guilt
Of all the trees that they chopped down.
And now you're lying in your hospital bed
Blagging fags off all your guests
With your bubbling lungs
And your yellow vest.
Will you be right glad?
Will you feel it in your chest?
Your life was made of fags

As you struggle for your last breath.
They never taught you knots at school
So you can't tie a noose,
And you can't afford a shotgun
And Bic razors just won't do it,
And the oven is electric
And you haven't got a car,
The trains are unreliable
The nearest cliff to far,
So just have another fag
Oh they're worse for you than scag,
And you'll die horribly
A coughing cursing hag.

Formica

Look at me I'm very happy
Watching my square box T V,
Eating my square box TV dinner
In my rabbit hutch house
On a Brookside street.
I twitch my nets at the neighbours
They twitch their nets back at me,
I wonder what the milkman could be doing
To the woman
At number 23?

I bought new white kitchen worktops
I've wanted them all of my life,
My wife she managed to damage them
So I carved her up with a knife,
You can blame violence on drugs or the telly,
You can blame it on just what you like,
I know it's because Formica
Is beautiful and shiny and white.

I buried my wife in the garden
My neighbours think that she left me,
They don't know I am a nutter
Capable of murder
In the first degree.
I killed her cos I didn't like her,
I traded her in for Formica,
It doesn't nag
It doesn't refuse to shag
And it's beautifully wipe clean and whiter.

I love it here in suburbia
Nobody here questions me,
I go to church every Sunday
And I've got the cleanest car on the street,
So I think I'll lie low here in suburbia,

In my rabbit hutch house hat I've bought,
And hope nobody digs up the garden
Cos it'll never stand up in the court
When I say...

I killed her cos I didn't like her
I traded her in for Formica,
It doesn't nag
It doesn't refuse to shag
And it's beautifully wipe clean and whiter.

Evil twin

When I woke up this morning
Everything was broken,
My head was hurt
All I could taste was gin,
My friends they just looked at me
And not a word was spoken,
But it was not me
It was my evil twin.
My evil twin she's big and bad
And booze makes her go mad
She falls around and terrorizes boys,
They don't want to be her lover
And they all run for cover
Cos she's very drunk
And makes an awful noise.

My evil twin she just arrives
She don't need to be invited,
She'll break the doors if you don't let her in.
She's obnoxious when she drinks
She'll probably throw up in your sink,
And then she'll swear she can't remember anything.
My evil twin she's big and bad
And booze makes her go mad,
She'll nick everything that isn't bolted down,
Her pockets are all bulging
And yet she's still indulging,
Grab her quick and lock her in the pound.

Well my life is such a shame
Cos I always get the blame
For all the evil sins my twin commits,
You think I've dropped a clanger
But it was my doppelgänger
And I'm the one who ends up getting hit.

My evil twin she's large as life
She's trouble and she's strife
She's about as base as anyone could ever be,
She's like a rabid dog
And I'll never get a snog.
As long as all the world's convinced that she is me.

Himalayas

World very big
Tree very tall
Moon small disc
Steep valley roar
With river
And jungle.
Monkey and more
Birds singing their praises
To the earth here
Than rocks
In the riverbed
Rattling in the depths
Of my sleep.
Keep in my heart
The deep green smell of paradise,
Dripping moss on rocks,
In a jungle,
In a valley,
In the foothills,
Of the mountains,
On the earth.

Hippy song

You ain't no brother of mine brother,
I grew up with two and I don't need others,
You won't want to be in my family
When you hear what I've got to sing
You ain't no brother of mine brother.

You ain't no brother of mine brother
Stop singing songs about my mother,
You're a yoghurt overload
And you look a bit like a toad
You ain't no brother of mine brother.

You ain't no sister of mine sister
If you disappeared I wouldn't miss ya,
Oh I won't drink your hippy tea
Even if it's good for me,
You ain't no sister of mine sister.

Holding hands in circles really makes me sick,
I'd like to lamp you with your talking stick,
You'd better make sure that you're aligned
Or you might get a punch in your third eye
You ain't no brother of mine brother.

I hope your tipi leaks in the rain
Because you live in Wales and not an Indian plain,
You'd better learn to pay that drum
Or I'm gonna stick it up your bum
You ain't no brother of mine brother.

You ain't no brother of mine brother
Stop singing songs about my mother,
Oh what's she ever done to you?
Murders what I'm gonna do
If you don't stop singing songs about my mother.

Blagging

I'm just a girl who can't say no
If you're giving it away I'll give it a go,
I can eat anything you know
And can I have a swig of brandy?
Give us a go on your special brew
You look quite tasty can I have a go on you?
I'll be the first in your dinner queue
And can I have a swig of brandy?

Can I skin up with your blim?
Is that your baccy in that tin?
Have you got a spare safety pin
And can I have a swig of brandy?
You'd better keep your eye on me,
Or I'll be in your bed and fast asleep
And then I'll pocket all your herbal tea
And finish off your brandy.

I'll eat the contents of your fridge,
I'll tat the plastic off your kids
Then I'll move into your garage,
Go on lend us a quid and I'll buy some more brandy.
Yes I know the meaning of thrift
Are you driving somewhere?
Can I have a lift?
Shame I've got nothing to be thrifty with
Apart from other people's brandy.

Boyfriends

So now your quiet life is getting lairy,
And all your boyfriends are converging in one place,
And the sight of them on mass is fairly scary,
Oh it puts a smirk of terror on your face.
Well you never realised you had so many,
And what possessed them all to come today?
Maybe it's time to go out in disguise
Or maybe it's time to run away...

My guilt has got me making up excuses,
My loins are fuelled by ecstasy and booze,
My hormones are rampaging
And your pheromones enraging
And I've only got cheap underwear to loose.
Not to worry you can always get six others,
If this batch aren't suitably impressed,
And maybe these six others
Will have brothers,
And they'll all be
Good in bed.

Supermarket song

Oh it was on the edge of town
Where the fields were green and bright,
They built a great big supermarket
And it looked like a pile of shite.
You have to go there in your car
Cos it's so far away from town,
And you haven't any choices
Cos all the other shops shut down.

The staff are miserable as sin
The food irradiated plastic,
And they lock up all their bins
And the expense is quite fantastic.
It's good to go with empty pockets,
It's good to go with fingers light,
It's good to swipe those special offers,
Cos major profit making's shite.

What is going on?

People starving in their millions,
People spending all their billions,
Plastic bags in their trillions
What is going on?

People shopping
Til they're dropping,
People eating
Til they're popping,
People dying for your shopping
What is going on?

People selling
People buying
People fighting
People dying,
World Bank profits terrifying
What is going on?

People bleeding in their fetters
Making someone a bit fatter,
Always someone getting battered
What is going on?

Gardening job

I like trees
But not that one
Because it spreads
Its leaves
On my lawn.
Chop it down
And while you're out there
Get those daisies.
Their freedom to grow
Offends me,
And each morning
Their sweet faces mock me
As I strangle myself with my tie.

Sailing By

(Accompanied by the tune 'Sailing By' from the shipping forecast)

The future is looking quite bleak
The sea is getting more deep,
It's encroaching,
Take up boating,
Or just hope your sofa starts floating.
You can build a big ark
If you work in the dark,
No one will see you and laugh (ha ha ha).
Rats and squirrels are easy to find,
But it's more difficult for giraffes.

The tide is rising high
Oh no we're all going to die,
It's futile, wearing armbands
You better start waving goodbye.
You can build a big ark
If you work in the dark,
No one will see you and laugh (ha ha ha).
Rats and squirrels are easy to find,
But it's more difficult for giraffes.

Where will England be
When there's no more BBC?
No more faffing
With the tuning
Because London is under the sea.
Wave goodbye
Sailing by,
You'd better start waving goodbye.
Wave goodbye
Sailing by,
I'm taking up sailing
Goodbye.

NIMBY

We do love your lifestyle
Unconventional ideals
And untimely arrivals
But not just here.

Could you just move a few miles to the
Left/right
North/south
Out of sight
Over there.

We really admire your wandering spirit
Especially when it is
Elsewhere.

Love poem

I am like the wind
I disappear
I turn
I return
I derange
I re-appear,
Blow hot and cold
I am here
I am not here,
I arrive in a certain place
One direction
Once a year,

If I love you
You may hear my song on the wind
Although I am long gone

New life
(2002-2007)

Pregnant

My sharp wit
Vanished into
Big tits.
My trousers don't fit.
My memory became mammary,
My bra's not big enough
My reversing skills killed themselves
My brain is growing fluff.
I can't drink,
Smoke,
Think,
Take drugs or jokes,
I no longer like blokes.

What am I?

Baby song

I've stopped drinking endless coffees
And I've started staying in,
I've quit smoking ciggies
And I've given up the gin,
I've dropped the string of boyfriends
Whose hearts I could never win,
Cos Lord Jesus Christ has sent me a little baby for my sins.

I've seen the light from heaven and now Jesus is my crutch.
I understand the Bible it's no longer double Dutch,
I believe in miracles since I've felt his heavenly touch
It really is a miracle one so small could shit so much.

I no longer need to live in sin to keep awake at night,
I don't wear frilly knickers,
I don't gamble
I don't fight,
So grateful to be rescued from my immortal plight
Cos I know that Jesus loves me though I smell of baby shite.

I'd like to thank Lord Jesus Christ for sweet sleep deprivation,
The row of stitches in my arse,
Sore nipples and dehydration,
I've heard it said that good motherhood is the making of the nation,
I'd better put my baby in a box
And leave him at the station.

I want to give birth to a clanger because clangers are made of pink wool.

I want to give birth to a clanger
Because clangers are made of pink wool,
They were knitted by Oliver's auntie
And they don't shit and vomit or bawl,
Their faces are streamlined and pointy
And they never cause trouble at all,
Oh it wouldn't be such a big problem
To squeeze one from such a small hole.

Instead I gave birth to a baby
With a head like a giant football,
And when he arrives he was screaming
But I screamed the loudest of all,
Humans are full of design faults
The biggest of all is in mums,
Cos for about sixteen weeks after
I couldn't sit down on my bum.

I want my brain back

Where's my brain gone?
Used to write all those songs with it,
And it wasn't rock and roll that made it vanish,
It could be a pumpkin,
Or maybe the big bad wolf blew it away,
But it's probably in a box of old toys in a garage.
I want my brain back,
All rusty and dusty and covered with bits,
I want my brain back,
I'm considering using it
To write something witty,
With lyrics to die for,
And a tune you can dance to,
About some amazing event that's affecting the planet,
It won't make number one
It'll be far too intellectual,
It'll rhyme
It'll scan
It'll have lots of clever bits in it.
I want my brain back, all rusty and dusty and covered in bits,
I want my brain back,
I'm considering using it.

I want my brain back
Before it's too late,
I want my brain back
Before it reaches its sell by date
Which is stamped on the bottom,
I want my brain back.

Duck cow tractor

And now the baby's gone to bed
He's laid to rest his sleepy head
And I can sit about instead of changing dirty nappies.
I've had a glass of wine
And I am feeing kind of silly,
And I play my ukulele
Cos I haven't got a willy.

Today we played on the swings
And then with lots of plastic things
And oh the joy that childhood brings
Is mindless yet delightful.
I'll be in my bed by nine
If I have another glass of wine,
Cos motherhood is the new rock and roll
Yeah.

Ooooooooooo
My communicational skills are regressing,
Ooooooo
It's depressing,
Ooooooo
Duck cow tractor
Quack broom moo.

Two little dickie birds sitting on a wall
One name Peter one named Paul,
Fly away Peter fly away Paul,
Come back Peter come back Paul.
Incy Wincey spider climbing up the spout,
Down came the rain and washed poor Incy out,
Out came the sunshine and dried up all the rain,
So Incy Wincey spider climbed up the spout again.

Oooooo
Duck cow tractor

Quack broom mooo,
Round and round the garden
Like a teddy bear,
I only know four chords
It's all I've had the time for
Oooooo

Sweat shop

Now listen carefully girls and boys
If you don't put away your toys,
Or if you trash your brand-new shoes,
Or if you're making too much noise,
Your parents might just have enough
And reach the point on which they snap,
Then it's the Nike factory for you.
It's the Nike factory for you,
It's the Nike factory for you,
You can work for fifteen hours a day
Making shoes for the world on a very low pay,
So some retailer in the west
Can put on pounds inside his vest,
I think they call that slavery
I think they call that slavery
It's the Nike factory for you.

If you're a greedy screaming brat
And you keep hassling that cat,
Or if you leave your coat behind,
Or you refuse to wear that hat,
Your parents might just have enough
And reach the point on which they snap,
Then watch it or its Persian rugs for you.
Watch it or its Persian rugs for you,
Watch it or its Persian rugs for you,
Ten children locked in one small room
To lose their fingers on the loom
So some fat salesman in the west
Can put on pounds inside his vest,
I think they call that slavery
I think they call that slavery,
Watch it or its Persian rugs for you.

If you refuse to go to bed
Or clout your best mate round the head,

If you don't share those sweeties out,
Or if that hamster don't get fed,
Your parents might just have enough
And reach the point on which they snap,
Then watch it or its cocoa beans for you.
Watch it or its cocoa beans for you,
Watch it or its cocoa beans for you,
A major African industry
More profitable than ivory
Where you can work all day for free
For chocolate that you'll never see,
So some fat kiddie in the west
Can put on pounds inside his vest,
And his parents can eat chocolate bars
Whilst driving around in fancy cars,
I think they call that slavery,
I think they call that slavery,
Watch it or its cocoa beans for you.

Home on the range

Oh give me a home
Where the washing up's done
Where the carpets get clean by themselves.
Where all that is heard
Is the occasional word
From those magical, cleaning up elves.
Home, home on the range,
Where I don't have to cook my own tea.
They pick up my knickers
And wash my old socks,
Oh those elves really do it for me.

Relentless life
(2008-2015)

This land is...

This land's not your land,
This land's not my land,
So lend me fifty grand
And I'll buy some woodland,
I'll stick a trailer there
And live without a care
Until the council come and kick me off.

My neighbours hate me,
They think I'm smelly,
They think I don't wash
Or have a telly,
And every weekend is wild party,
As I stay at home listen to radio 4 and drink tea
(Oh God how boring).
All I want is a peaceful life,
Kettles and veg and a good sharp knife,
A decent shovel and somewhere to shit,
A nice warm trailer with a sofa to sit on,
Don't want to live in a house in a town,
Don't want idiots hanging around,
Don't want a fight,
Don't want a fright,
All I want is a peaceful life.
But this land's not your land,
This land's not my land,
So lend me fifty grand
And I'll buy some woodland,
I'll stick a trailer there
And live without a care
Until the council come and kick me off.

New nuclear

In an overcrowded island
In the northern hemisphere,
Our great leaders have decided
That the way is nuclear,
As in all great democracies
There's been no debate about it,
It's a forgone conclusion and your rights are being flouted,
But how did we used to live without sixteen showers a day,
And badly made electrical goods that we use then chuck away?
How did we live without chocolate fondues or machines for making bread?
We must have done it somehow or else we'd all be dead.

But we don't have to clean it up
We're going to leave a mess
So future generations can deal with the stress
Of toxic waste sat in the ground
Cos we don't give a toss,
As long as our fridge is as big as an airship
And our telly's the size of a bus.

Why can't our power supply be localised?
A village with a wind turbine could be a source of pride,
Our roofs could be made of solar, we could harvest the incoming tide,
But fuck it, let's go with nuclear and trash the countryside
Because we don't have to clean it up
We're going to leave a mess
So future generations can deal with the stress
Of toxic waste sat in the ground
Cos we don't give a toss,
As long as our fridge is as big as an airship
And our telly's the size of a bus.

Diamond geezer

My mind is blank
My urges dank
My ships all sank
My life is wank.

Can't keep a job
Can't leave the mob
Can't find my knob
Can't shut my gob.

Caused lots of strife
Pissed off my wife
Fucked off my friends
Fucked up my life,

So here I sit
Like a fat git
Drinking beer,
And talking shit.

Garden shed not bloodshed

If BAE systems made slug traps
Rather than weapons of war,
Instead of collateral damage
There'd be carrots and cabbage galore,
If Lockheed Martin were busy
Tending their wildflower lawn,
There'd be no time left to make spy planes,
Stealth fighters and nuclear bombs.

If everyone planted a fruit bush
On the land that was their birth right,
They'd be so busy stuffing their faces with fruit
There'd be no time left over to fight,
Instead of land mines
Could be planted grape vines
At least people would only get legless on wine,
We could work something out,
A solution would sprout
On gardeners question time.

If suicide bombers were armed with
A hoe and a rake and some seeds,
Instead of slaughtering infidels
They could concentrate on the weeds,
Alive and content at the end of the day
Scraping the mud from their shoes,
If Hitler'd been busy manuring his leeks,
Would he have killed six million Jews?

The B.N.P. song

Founded by a neo-Nazi
It used to be called the National Front,
Now it has the facade of an electable party
When really they're just a bunch of criminals and thugs.
What's the point in living if we can't learn from history?
What if fascists surf to power
On a big wave of apathy?

Indigenous white Briton is a mythical creature
Like a nice Tory
Or a unicorn,
Or a dragon in a cave
Or a normal teacher,
Or a perpetual motion generator
Providing free electricity
From magnetic energy,
I've seen them on the internet for £99.50,
And they're about as likely to work
As B.N.P. policy
On immigration
Or industry
Or education.

Just how do you define a native Briton?
Is it a Roman or a Viking
A Saxon or a Frenchman?
How far back do you want to take immigration?
You can't repatriate a mongrel nation.
They want to wrap us up in parcel tape
And send us back in time,
Instead of a postcode
We'll all have a bloodline.
60 million parcels marked return to sender,
60 million parcels sent back 60 millennia,
Arriving at the feet of the first people
Who walked out of Africa.

Because when we bleed we all bleed red,
We're pink inside
Our tears are wet
And when we get hurt people who love us get upset,
And when we die we're dead
That's a fact.

CCTV

Out for a picnic with your lovely family
Get a bit of shopping, cross a road and drink some tea,
Sitting in a pub or waiting for a public loo
Somebody's watching you.
Stopping at the lights or going round a roundabout,
Driving down the road or parking up and getting out,
 Whizzing down a motorway or sitting in a queue,
Somebody's watching you.
Yes someone is watching you
No you're not being paranoid
There's CCTV everywhere
It's something that you can't avoid,
Filming every sneeze and every scratch and every yawn
And someone poor low paid bastard has to sit and watch it all.

Sitting on a bench or walking doggy down the street,
Every stranger passing you or matey that you meet,
Every step you take and every boring thing you do,
Somebody's watching you.
Every shop you enter, every cash point you frequent,
Every bus and every train and everywhere you went,
In the dead of night or sunny Sunday afternoon,
Somebody's watching you.
Yes someone is watching you
No you're not being paranoid
There's CCTV everywhere
It's something that you can't avoid,
Like fishes in a fish-tank, or monkeys at the zoo
Somebody's watching you.

Yes someone is watching you
No you're not being paranoid
There's CCTV everywhere
It's something that you can't avoid,
Just in case a hoodie comes to get you with a knife,
At least if you get stabbed to death someone will watch you die.

Real love song

Oh my lover is shrinking,
His teeth are falling out his head,
And his hairline is receding
Though that's better left unsaid.
Slouching in his smeggy long-johns,
Spilling Horlicks in the bed,
But you'd be fools to believe
That the passion is dead.
 Though we only get to do it once a month
If we manage not to fall asleep,
It's more enjoyable
Than counting sheep.

First the dailies turn into the weeklies,
Then the weeklies turn into the monthlies,
Then the monthlies only happen
If we're not too tired and grumpy.
Oh but I love my man
And I couldn't ask for more,
I hope we get to do it annually
By the age of 94,
 Though we'll only get to do it
Once a year,
Our love is gonna keep out the chill
As death draws near.

Stop it

Stop buying things
Things are crap,
You don't need things,
Things cost money.
Even if a thing is 99p,
100 things aren't cheap.
Could stay at home and just eat rice,
Look at the sky
The sky looks nice,
Deep breathe
Climb a tree,
Shag
Snog
Snooze
Pee.
Lie in the grass,
Swim in the sea,
Sit on your arse
With a flask full of tea,
All those things are fun
And they are free.
I can walk
Walking is free
Exercise without a gym fee,
I can talk cos talking is free,
And I can think because thought is free,
I can go to the park
The park is free,
Sit in the dark
The dark is free,
I can eat food I find for free
I can dance at a free party.

I can love
Because love is free
Though that is bullshit
Obviously,
Love comes at the highest price
But who cares
Because it's love
And it is nice.

Forty and fat

I'd never heard of control underwear
Til I found myself forty and fat,
I thought you just bought the next size up
If you couldn't squeeze into that.
I don't care if my tits hit my nose
When I do the headstand yoga pose,
And I don't care that I can't see my toes
Because I like beer and that's how it goes.
But the adverts told me
That I'd be an old maid,
That would never get lucky
And never get laid,
And my teeth will decay, and my beauty will fade,
And I won't get a job, and I'll never get paid
So I bought some.

So now when you see me I'm looking quite svelte
And sassy and sexy and fit,
Don't go undressing me with your eyes
Underneath I look like a twit,
I'm wearing beige pants that come up to my armpits,
They'd have any reasonable suitor in fits,
And I'm turning bright red because I'm over-heating a bit.

The reason behind my story and the moral behind this tale,
Don't squeeze yourself in a small spandex tube
And then consume 6 pints of ale,
You can't stand you can't breathe
You can't think you can't cough,
You can't laugh you can't dance
You can't drink you can't scoff,
And if you find a man, drag him home and cop off,
You'll need sixteen mates around to shoehorn them off
And that will scare him.

So I'm not wearing control underwear
Now I find myself forty and fat,
I think I'll just buy the next size up
And happily squeeze into that.
I'll celebrate that my tits hit my nose
When I do the headstand yoga pose,
And I'll keep making sure that I can't see my toes
Because I like beer and that's how it goes.

Car boot sale (a song written on a 1960's electric accordion that I bought at the car boot sale).

If you're sick of boring Sundays,
You can go and have a fun day
By frequenting the car boot sale.
If you think that God is boring,
And you're really into hoarding,
Then just go to the car boot sale.
You can buy a cheap guitar,
Or a hot wheels car,
Or a load of handy jars,
Or some bananas.
The choices that you make depend what gender and what age you are,
Will you buy the stack of readers wives?
Or the old foot spa?
All you've ever wanted from the back of someone's car
And you can buy it at the car boot sale.

You can buy some cheap meat
Off the cheap meat man,
He's got a microphone
And he's from Birmingham.
You can buy a side of bacon as a present for your Nan,
And still have enough money left to buy a frying pan,
All you've ever wanted from the back of someone's van
And you can buy it at the car boot sale.

If you're unhappy, or feel ignored,
If you suffer from depression
Or you're just quite bored,
You can snaffle a quick burger and then go out and maraud,
Murdering the masses with your cheapo, repro sword,
All you've ever wanted, from someone else's hoard,
And you can buy it at the car boot sale.

If you're a musician
That is quite poor,
You could shop at the booty
For instruments galore,
Like this fine accordion
Made in 1964,
So I can still play music, though I can't stand up no more,
And when I'm in my nineties
I can still go out on tour,
And I bought it at the car boot sale.

Fit for Armageddon

So now I have taken up running
To beat my middle age spread,
And I'm in training for Armageddon
Cos the fastest looters always get fed,
So although you are walking faster than me
And I am turning bright red,
In the end
I will be running and you will be dead.
What will Armageddon be?
Will Jesus Christ come down to judge me?
Or will zombies eat my brains for tea?
Will the world flood, or a mixture of the three?
So although you are walking faster than me
And I am turning bright red,
In the end
I will be running and you will be dead.

So now I have taken up skiing
To beat the avalanche of doom
Coming my way,
And it's a very impractical habit
For an English person on a very low wage.
My movements aren't fluid or graceful,
And my arms flap about in the air,
But as long as I can beat the grim reaper
Why should I care?
What will Armageddon be?
Will Jesus Christ come down to judge me?
Or will zombies eat my brains for tea?
Will the world flood, or a mixture of the three?
My movements aren't fluid or graceful,
And my arms flap about in the air,
But as long as I can beat the grim reaper
Why should I care?

So now I have taken up swimming
And I'll be able to float like the ark,
And like most middle aged women in a costume
I look lumpy and droopy and better in the dark,
But come the final judgement
With my swimming hat firm on my head,
I will be swimming
And you, you will be dead.
What will Armageddon be?
Will Jesus Christ come down to judge me?
Or will zombies eat my brains for tea?
Will the world flood, or a mixture of the three?
But come the final judgement,
With my swimming hat firm on my head,
I will be swimming
And you, you will be dead.

Idioms

In the blink of an eye
Your life will pass you by,
It'll fit on the head of a pin,
Can you cram it all in?
Because you don't want to get to the dock
To find that your ship has sailed,
In the shake of a tail
The days slip by.
So get your ducks in a row,
Get your show on the road,
Hit the ground at a run
Find your moment
In the sun,
Live large, live life like a king,
It's sink or swim,
Give it your best shot,
One life is all you've got.
Because
In the blink of an eye
Your life will pass you by,
It'll fit on the head of a pin,
Can you cram it all in?
Because you don't want to get to the dock
To find that your ship has sailed,
In the shake of a tail
The days slip by.

When you croak
When you drop off the twig,
Pop your clogs, kick the bucket, bite the dust,
When you've breathed your last
And you're looking at the other side of the grass,
When you've shuffled off this mortal coil,
Sold the farm and called it a day,
I hope you kicked life's butt
From the cradle to the grave,

Because
In the blink of an eye
Your life will pass you by,
It'll fit on the head of a pin,
Can you cram it all in?
Because you don't want to get to the dock
To find that your ship has sailed,
In the shake of a tail,
The days slip by.

February Poem

Dying, we're all dying
Some quicker than others
And anyone who says they're not dying
Is lying.

But while we're not quite dead
We're still living,
Launching offspring
Despatching parents
Worrying,
Working,
Gardening,
Giving,
To keep all bellies full
And all heads above water.

Retaining some perspective
Finding some joy
Keeping some semblance of personal freedom,
Some spark, some thriving
In the living
Part of dying

Don't Google that lump

Don't google that growth,
Don't google that bump,
Don't google that pustulant boil,
That wheeze, or that sneeze or that lump.
Cos you will find
That you're going to die,
Painfully and horribly
Without the time to ask why.
In about three days
Your legs will drop off,
Your heart will fail, your head will explode
So don't google that cough.

Your hair will fall out
Your teeth will fall in,
Your nose will drop off
And be chucked in a bin.
Your spleen will implode
Your lungs will explode,
You'll become a quadruple amputee
Or someone who's experienced a lobotomy.
You will never walk again
A thousand tiny spiders will hatch from your brain,
You will go insane
So don't google that pain.

So now you've got cancer
And HPV,
Rheumatoid arthritis, osteoporosis, insomnia and COPD
You're developing Alzheimer's and you're severely depressed,
Hyper-tense and menopausal
Jesus you're a mess.
You've got fifteen separate STD's, swine flu and kidney disease
E bola's gonna see you off
Don't google that cough.

I know

I know where the lazy fox catches the last rays of evening sun.
I know where
Butterfly orchid, crab apple and damson grow.
I know where badgers drink ,
Owls hunt
And deer sleep in the day,
I know each twisting way through the wood.

 I am an encyclopaedia of all my family's needs,
Finding shoes and wallets,
Lost toys, glasses, glue,
Scissors, paper, keys,
But I don't know
Where the dead go,
Or how to fill the hole
That is shaped like you.

Come run away with me

Come run away with me
Let's be poets together
Then we can live in luxury
Up our own arses forever.

Thanks

An especially big thankyou to Lucy Peacock for knowing how to make a book and get it to the printers, it wouldn't ever have happened without you – I'll listen to your poetry anytime and I owe you about 25 curries.

Another big thankyou to Kate Evans for being the best cartoonist ever, knowing how Photoshop works and being a very good friend.

The biggest love to my tiny family of two. It makes me cry thinking about how much I love you.

Thanks to my lovely dog for ensuring I have to leave the house at least once a day and can never become a recluse.

Thanks to my Dutch and Portuguese friends who I miss - I come around for imaginary drinks at your places on most days.